NO MATTER WHAT

NO MATTER WHAT

and other poems

JERMAINE EMMANUEL CROCKETT

ISBN-13: 9781530581474
ISBN-10: 1530581478

NO MATTER WHAT

No matter what you do,
Good or bad, people will always hate you.

Everybody wants to hate;
Nobody wants to appreciate.
When you eat, they hope you choke and suffocate.

No matter what you do,
Good or bad, they will never be thankful.
They want to see you upset and miserable.

No matter what happens,
Don't let them in.
Don't let them win.

No matter what you do,
Good or bad, people will always hate you.

MY DEEPEST THOUGHTS

Rain falls on the windowpane once again.
My deepest thoughts are about an old friend
And how all good things must come to an end.

As the rain falls, my deepest thoughts are about the past
And how time moves so fast
When you're happy and having a blast.

As the rain falls, my deepest thoughts are about the missed opportunities
And stepping out of my comfort zone and breaking boundaries;
My deepest thoughts are about the things that stop me from being me.
Rain falls down on the windowpane once again;
My deepest thoughts come to an end.

MOUNTAIN GIRL

She lives in the mountains; the cold air is her friend,
And the high view that never comes to an end.

She looks down below at the rooftops
And the city people that never stop,
Always working around the clock.

She stands on the mountain ground;
The sound of birds and nature is her favorite sound,
The air so clean, no pollution around.

She lives in the mountains, happy and free,
The way life is supposed to be.

LONELY STREET

He walks the streets alone;
Thanks to his mum, he's now looking for a new home.

It's raining,
But he carries on walking;
There seems to be no end to his suffering.

He rests underneath a bus shelter
To protect himself from the horrible weather.
He reaches into his pocket and takes a look at the family picture,
Then continues the never-ending adventure,
Not knowing where the road will take him;
Life for him never seemed so grim.

He walks the streets alone;
Thanks to his mum, now he has to make it on his own.

HAIR IN PIGTAILS

She has her hair in pigtails.
Her nice-smelling fragrance leaves a trail;
Her beauty attracts all males.

She walks in high heels but not too high,
An umbrella over her head to keep her dry,
All eyes on her as she walks on by.

The guys look but don't make it too obvious.
She know she has an audience,
But she plays oblivious.

She has her hair in pigtails.
Her nice-smelling fragrance leaves a trail;
Her beauty attracts all males.

She walks into the horizon,
Never to be seen again.

LAST NIGHT'S PAIN

Like a ghost he was gone,
Gone before the morning came.
She was left wondering what she'd done,
Wondering how it went from right to wrong.

No text, no call,
Nothing at all,
Just a pile of her own clothes on her floor.

Lying naked in bed,
A thousand thoughts running through her head,
Wondering if she should try dating girls instead.

She gets up and starts the day,
Hoping her pain and thoughts go away.

Like a ghost he was gone,
Gone before the morning came.
When he walked out the door, he knew he'd done wrong.

He didn't text,
He didn't call,
He gave her no explanation at all.

He thought about calling her,
But his finger wouldn't type the number.
At the same time, he had the fear she might answer.

Here comes the sun;
A new day has begun,
But he's still ashamed of what he has done.

GHOST TOWN

It's a complete ghost town,
Nobody around.
I'm listening; I can't hear a sound.

No women, no men, no boys, no girls,
No litter, no noise.

Where did everyone go?
Who did they follow?
An angel or a devil?
Something happened; was it good or was it evil?
The streets are empty.
There's nobody around me.
I feel so scared, so lonely.

Where is everybody?
Why did they leave me?

I don't understand why
They never say good-bye.

LIFE CHALLENGES

She sits alone by the window,
Her heart full of misery and sorrow,
Fearful of the trouble that will come tomorrow.

She stares at the window and watches the rain.
She doesn't see water droplets; she see a distraction from the pain.
But the rain stops, and the reality comes back round again.
As time goes past,
Her eyes are still fixed on the glass,
Wondering why life is full of challenges and hard tasks.

She sits alone by the window,
Her heart full of misery and sorrow,
But there is something she doesn't know:
The challenge in life is to let our troubles go.

COCAINE

Why is it when you're having fun,
Life comes around and bites you on the bum?
To make things worse, you run out of whisky or rum.

Now you have nothing to block the pain,
Nothing to stop you from going insane,
And you're three years clean of cocaine.

You have loads of problems,
And you have no idea how to solve them.

On top of that, your wife wants a divorce and wants the home,
And she won custody of the kids, so now you're all alone.
Divorce costs money, and the bank won't give you a loan.
Wife, soon to be ex-wife, is calling you, but you refuse to pick up the phone.

You solve one problem, but it comes back again.
You still have nothing to block out the pain;
You still have nothing to stop you from going insane.
After three years, you give up; it's time to go back to cocaine.

BAD ORPHANAGE

They're watching me, they're watching you,
They're watching everything we do,
Their eyes fixed on us like glue.

Their eyes we can't escape;
Every day we feel like a cape.
The boys prepare for a beating; the girls prepare for rape.

Nowhere to run, nowhere to hide, we're stuck.
Life for us sucks;
I guess this is the definition of bad luck.

Every day we hope for a hero to save us,
To break free from this undeserved curse,

But that never happens;
We carry on, getting mistreated until our life ends.

ADDICTED

Addicted to money, addicted to power—
To him that's all that matters.
It helps him stand strong like a tower.
Due to a weak foundation, he topples over.

Addicted to money, addicted to power—that's what completes him.
Addicted to money, addicted to power—that's his problem.
Addicted to money, addicted to power—that's what made him a victim.

People watched him rise; now they will watch him fall.
The people watched him get everything; now they watch him lose it all.
The people respected him; the people don't respect him anymore.

Now he walks along the land,
Not as a leader but as a simple man.

BEACH GIRL

She's a beach girl; she loves the sound of the sea.
She's a beach girl; she loves the cool breeze.
It makes her feel at ease.

She's a beach girl; she walks barefoot on the sand,
Sunglasses on her face and an ice-cream cone in her hand.
She lives near the beach, where all her troubles are banned.

She walks along the shore, getting her feet a little wet,
At the same time admiring the sunset.
She lives near the beach, where life is simple, not complex.

She's a beach girl
Where the sun, sand, and sea are so beautiful.

COWGIRL AND COWBOY

He's a cowboy, she's a cowgirl,
They both live happily in a miserable world,
Drinking cold beer in the summer and whisky when it gets cold.

Living in a small shack,
Traveling together on horseback,
Their love is solid, no cracks.

They grew up in the small town
Where there were horses and big fields all around.
An acoustic guitar with a slow rhythm is their favorite sound.

She's a cowgirl and he's a cowboy;
Living happily in a miserable world is what they both enjoy.

BALL OF FIRE

We watch with restful but open eyes
As the ball of fire burns the skies.
The people watch as the day slowly dies.

After today's struggles, we take a moment
And watch, full of enjoyment.
After today's troubles, we're glad that we got through it.

The ball of fire in the sky burns low,
Leaving behind a beautiful glow
And putting on a wonderful show.

DARK SIDE

High five.
Welcome to the dark side.
Together we come alive.

Abandon all hope before you come in;
You're a loser, so don't expect to win.

They hated you;
They treated you like a fool.
They're so mean and uncool.

Come and join us.
We are the people you can trust;
We won't leave you in the dust;
We will put you first.

Welcome to the dark side.
We will make you feel alive.

DOWNFALL

The rain starts to pour;
The thunder starts to roar;
High waves crash against the shore;
The birds no longer soar;
I guess this is the downfall of us all.

The days are dark and the clouds are gray;
All the happiness in the world has gone away.
No one told us that our happiness was here to stay.
Who knows if it will come back another day?
Who knows what the future holds?
Will better days come tomorrow?
Or will it bring sorrow?

The rain starts to pour;
The thunder starts to roar;
Cracks run deep along the floor;
This must be the downfall of us all.

FOULMOUTHED BOYS

Here come those foulmouthed boys,
Causing trouble and making too much noise;
Giving old ladies a fright is what they enjoy.

They sleep all day,
But they come out at night to play.
Everybody in the neighborhood wants them to stay away.

They set the residents' cars on fire.
They watch, full of happiness and laughter,
As the cars burn; their smiles get brighter.

The sunlight has shone;
The damage is done.
The foulmouthed boys are gone.

A NEW DAY

The moon is descending;
The sun is appearing;
A new day is coming;
It's time for the town's awakening.

From above the town is quiet and still.
What is this bad vibe I feel?
In the air there is a cold chill.
The sun is behind the clouds; darkness still remains.
The harsh cold night has left a tough stain.
Already their morning energy is drained.

The town has rested long enough,
But their bodies still feel rough.
A new day is here; get ready because this day is going to be tough.

A GIRL

They told her she wasn't powerful.
They told her she was just a girl,
A girl that walked through the darkness of the world,

Walked straight past evil,
Walked straight past trouble,
Walked straight past all obstacles.

Nothing dared get in her way
Because they knew she'd make them pay.

She was just a girl
Who walked through the darkness of the world
And forgot everything she was told.

GIRL IN THE DISTANCE

He saw her from afar;
Her smile shine bright like a star.
A beautiful woman in a miserable world—how bizarre.

He watched her from a distance,
Not knowing of her existence,
Hoping she would give him a quick glance.

She looked so beautiful,
Her face so wonderful;
She must be an angel.

She disappeared in the horizon.
He's wondering if he will see her again.

GAME OVER

She's running in fear;
She knows her attacker is near;
She doesn't want to be here.

She's stuck in a dark corner;
She wants to go home to her daughter.

She know she's about to get raped;
She tries to escape.

Her clothes come off one by one;
In under fifteen minutes, he is done.
To him it was a bit of fun;
Now he is on the run.

She cries in shame
Even though she's not to blame.
To the attacker it was a game;

Now the game is over.

HERO

He needed a hero
To save his soul.
He needed a hero
To save him from evil.

But heroes aren't real; they are only false illusions.
Now he walks around full of confusion,
Searching for a conclusion,

A conclusion to his struggles,
A conclusion to his troubles.

He searches high and low
Through the rain and snow

Until he comes to a mirror
And wonders,
Could he be the answer?

Could he be a hero
To help save his soul?
Could he be a hero
To help save himself from evil?

KING ALTER EGO

He has an alter ego;
It only comes out when he swallows alcohol.
When it comes out, the people are under his control.
He's not a leader, but they stand behind him and follow;
When he stands, they bow.

Just like a king they serve him,
Without any problem;
Whether it's an act of foolishness or wisdom,
They surround and protect him so he never becomes a victim.
He's not an outlaw; neither is he a part of the system.

Their lives revolve around this one man.
By his side they stand;
They feel lucky to live on the same land.
Why do people treat him like a king? That's something we don't understand.

He has an alter ego;
It only comes out when he swallows alcohol.
When it does, the people are under his control.
And as his people, they bow and follow;
To protect and serve—that is their vow.

PROSECCO

One week ago
An old lady from Glasgow
Brought me a bottle of prosecco,
And my family and I are so grateful.

It will go well with our dinner.
Our weight we don't think to consider,
Or how it will affect our figure.

We'll sit back and relax and enjoy the taste
As each and every one will have a smile on our face
Because the prosecco has made this home a better place.

One week ago
An old lady from Glasgow
Brought me a bottle of prosecco,
And I will remain forever grateful.

POLISH PEOPLE

I work with Polish people.
They treat me like an equal;
They are so cheerful and playful,

Always hardworking,
Full of positive thinking,
Giving their best in everything.

They're good at their job.
They work hard, nonstop.

I work with Polish people.
They treat me like an equal;
They make my job a bit more joyful.

RAINDROP

Raindrop on the windowpane,
White top covered in beer stains—
Foolish things help keep him entertained

Poor decisions lead to shame;
Good decisions don't always leads to fame.
Is life about opportunities or just a game?

Money doesn't always matter.
If it does, it will become your master:
Money comes, money scatters.

Raindrop on the concrete floor,
Poster hung up on the bedroom wall—
What goes on in the world won't matter anymore
As someone or something will end it all.

LEAVING SCHOOL

Leaving school can be a blessing or a curse.
It could be for the better or for the worse.

It can make you a winner
Or a loser.

Leaving school can make you smarter,
Or it can make you dumber.
Please believe me:
Leaving school is not easy,

But the path you choose
Is up to you.

MONSTER OR HUMAN

Drugs he uses;
Women he abuses;
In gambling games, he cheats so he never loses.

He is a monster
With so much power,
Bossing people around every minute, every hour.

He's not a god, but he feels like one.
Bullying people is his way of having fun;
Using other people is his way of getting things done.

Is there a reason why he acts this way?
Is this an act he puts on every day?

People want to knock him down,
But nobody knows his background.

Everybody wants to hate;
Nobody wants to appreciate.

Maybe we should be more understanding.
After all, he is human.

MORE MONEY

Isn't it funny
How people always want more money
Even when they have plenty?
The word "charity"
Is not in their vocabulary.

They say money can't buy you happiness,
So why do people try to start up their own business?
More money creates more problems and creates more laziness.

Pay bills and rent,
Buy beer and go to the strip club, and you say money well spent.
Wake up the next morning wondering where my money went.

Isn't it funny?
People always want more money
Even when they have plenty.

NOT GIRLFRIEND, NOT FOE

They come, they go,
Their names he doesn't know.
Not girlfriends, not friends, not foes.

He likes to live in the moment.
He can't help it;
He's an addict
But allergic to commitment.

He has no reasons.
The girls, they change just like the seasons.
They come, they go,
Not girlfriends, not friends, not foes

RICH MAN, POOR HEART

Rich man sitting on his money
While the poor man hasn't got any;
Rich man thinks it's funny.

Poor man begging for a glass of water;
All he has is a small shelter.
The rich man cries with laughter.

The poor man is humble.
His belly starts to rumble.
His leg hurts; he tries to walk, but he stumbles.

Have you got any spare change? he asks.
The rich man ignores him and walks past.
For the poor, eating a lovely meal is a hard task.

The rich man stands proud and tall
While he watches the poor man crawl
Along the dirty concrete floor.

The poor man is a winner; he is humble
And thankful

While the rich man cares more about his wealth
Than his health.

WHITE GLOSS PAINT

White gloss paint on the carpet—
The kids know who done it,
But they vowed to keep it a secret.

White is a lovely color,
But that doesn't matter;
Someone is going to bed without any supper.

The carpet is stained;
The kids are not ashamed.
All she wants is a name.

If it wasn't the kids, it must be the fairies.
They must have knocked it over during their secret party.

White gloss paint on the carpet—
Will she ever find out who done it?

BEST BEHAVIOR

He's on his best behavior,
Trying to impress her.
He's on his best behavior,
Trying to get her number.

Waiting for an opening,
Trying to keep the conversation flowing,
At the same time not giving useless information,

Like saying, I like trees,
Or I hate spiders and bumblebees.
Instead he remains focused,
Showing no signs of being nervous.
Inside he's shaking, but he looks calm on the surface.

He's on his best behavior,
Hoping it will pay off later.

DEMON

You guys always want to hate;
You guys never want to appreciate,
No matter if it's good or really great.

You refuse to understand
Only because we're not human,
Yet we never struck you with our hand.

Demon? Yes we are, but we're here to protect.
We save your lives, but you choose to forget.
Demon? Yes we are, but we still deserve your respect.

You will never treat us like equals;
Our lives will never be peaceful,
But we still protect you people,
Hoping one day you will call us heroes.

NATURE AND KIDS

Nature and kids—
What a perfect mix.
The kids sit on the grass to receive their sugar fix.

And when they're done,
They get up and carry on.
They jump; they play; they run;
They do whatever it takes to have fun.

They kick and throw the ball around;
They do this all day until the sun goes down,
All smiles, no frowns.

Nature and kids—what a perfect blend.
They go away as the day comes to an end,
But tomorrow they will do it all again.

GUNPOWDER

Gunpowder in the air,
Dead bodies everywhere,
And deep in her heart, she doesn't care.

She looks at the smoking gun;
She smiles at the work she has done.
She is proud of what she's become.

A criminal, a serial killer, and all of the above—
She dreamt of this moment when she was twelve.
Gunpowder in the air,
Dead bodies everywhere—
On the spot she stands there.
This time one of her eyes produces a tear.
The people shoot her down without any hesitation or fear.
She is dead; the people don't care.

EXPLORE THE WORLD

I've heard it once before,
Five hundred times or more:
The world is ours to explore.
But how can we when we have so much war?

How can we when we have famine and drought
And a solution we can't seem to figure out?
The people call for help, but we ignore their shouts.

How can we explore if we have bombs on planes?
How can we explore the streets if people are covered in bloodstains?
How can we explore when evil spreads through our veins?
How can we explore when violence is what goes on in our brains?

I've heard it once before,
Five hundred times or more:
The world was once ours to explore,
But not anymore.

DRUNK

He drank a lot; now he's ready to chat.
A fight's about to go down; where is his baseball bat?
He's not good at fighting, but he likes to ignore the facts.

He drank a lot; time to call his girlfriend and tell her he loves her.
When he wakes up, everything will be a blur.
All the stupid things he did he won't remember
Until he sees the pictures later.

She drank a lot, so she's getting emotional;
Excuse her if she becomes antisocial.
Ignore her if she tries to say you're beautiful.

He's drunk; time to get loud and hyper.
More shots of vodka
Followed by shots of tequila
And worry about the hangover later.

He's drunk, but he's not going to admit it,
So we all pretend he didn't vomit,
But at the end of the night, he still has his keys and wallet.

How will you act
When alcohol starts to attack?

THEIR LOVE

They found love on the platform,
An odd place, a bit out of the norm.
The weather is cold, but their love keeps them warm;
Their love is a shelter from the storm.

They found love on the side of the train track.
Same race, same height—opposites doesn't always attract.
Their love is natural, not an artifact;
Their love protects them from negative oncoming attacks.

Here comes the rain,
No sign of the train.
The warmth leaves their bodies, but their love still remains.
Their love is a distraction, so they don't complain.

To other people, their destination is unknown;
Their love for each other is shown.
Forever together and never alone—
Their love is strong as stone.

SELF-PITY

As time goes by slowly,
He sits in his room, full of self-pity,
Drowning his sorrow in a bottle of whisky.

He used to be strong,
But now he's lost the strength to carry on.

He's waiting, waiting for someone to save him,
Waiting for someone to help him with his problem,
But nobody can seem to find a solution.

As time goes by slowly,
He sits in his room, full of self-pity,
Wondering if he will ever be happy.

SUNRISE

Here come the sunrise.
It's time to open your eyes.
It's a new day; it took you some time to realize
The dream you had of the world is falsely advertised.

This is the real thing,
Where the birds are supposed to sing,

Where the air is polluted and unclean,
And the things you see have already been seen,
And the places you're going you've already been.

Time and time again,
You wait for a miracle to happen.

Instead of a miracle,
You get a never-ending cycle
That only ends when you're in a coffin and everyone's at your funeral.

GREAT SHAME

It went from good to bad,
From happy to sad;
He lost everything he had.

The question remains, how did he fall so hard?
Why did the crowd boo him? Why didn't they applaud?
Is this a punishment from God?

Everything went his way,
But suddenly the sky changed from blue to gray,
And everything he worked for went astray.
Now he walks full of dismay.

What a shame
To get this far and be taken out of the game.

MOONLIGHT

The moonlight shines on a quiet town,
A town where no footstep touches the ground,
A safe town where only good people hang around,
A town where people are safe and sound.

The moonlight shines on the green grass and rubbish bins;
The moonlight shines on buildings and things that move in the wind;
The moonlight shines on you and your friend.

The moonlight shines on her and him;
The moonlight has seen all your problems,
But the moonlight is not here to solve them.

You cannot escape the moonlight;
Forever it will keep you in its sight.

MORNING BATTLE

Here comes the sun.
Grab your gun;
The battle's begun.

Here comes the eight thirty alarm.
Turn it off and protect your ears from harm.

Second alarm's coming; take cover.
Quick, retreat to the shower;
Stay there till you gain power.

Get out; coast is clear.
Run to the bedroom and put on your gear.

Quick, to the kitchen; eat some porridge.
It will provide you with courage.
Now it's time to go out, all guns blazing, into the office.

You have to survive
The battle of nine-to-five.
Stand tall and be proud you're still alive.

Relax, open the beer bottle,
Because you have to do it all again tomorrow.

WE LIVE IN THIS WORLD

We live in this world with perverts and pedophiles.
We live in this world with stalkers with creepy smiles.
We live in this world with shameless people in denial.

We live in this world and watch the darkness grow.
Some days the darkness grows fast; some days it grows slow.
In some of us, the darkness grows from head to toe.

We live in this world with criminals
And humans that behave like animals.
We create things that are fictional
Because we don't want to see the bad things that are visible.

We live in this world
That is dark and cold,
And we die in this world
If we're young or old.

WE BOW OUR HEADS

We bow our heads in silence
To remember the night so violent,
To remember the death of the innocent.

We bow our heads and pray for peace.
We pray that the violence will not increase;
We pray for the ones that died in the streets.

We bow our heads and pray for the old and the young.
We bow our heads and pray for the ones that were having fun
As they will never see the rising of the morning sun.
We bow our heads and pray
To remember the violence that happened that day,
And in our prayers, the people will stay.

GRANDMA ALICE

Grandma Alice,
Old but full of advice.
Her kindness is free; there's no selling price.

When trouble comes, she'll be at your side;
Through the darkness, she'll be your guide;
A helping hand she will always provide.

Grandma Alice, a hero
From Glasgow
To pull us out of sorrow
And give us hope for tomorrow.

Grandma Alice, thank you
For everything you do.

Made in the USA
Charleston, SC
07 July 2016